36

THE STORY OF
Passover

by Norma Simon
illustrated by Erika Weihs

HarperCollins*Publishers*

For my cousins, Ruth and Jud, with much love
—NS

For Sophia, Joanna, Norah, and Leonora
—EW

The full-page illustrations in this book were done in oils on acid-free gesso-coated boards.
The jacket and borders were done in acrylics on acid-free boards.

The text for this book was first published in *Passover*, a Crowell Holiday Book edited by Susan Bartlett Weber, written by Norma Simon and illustrated by Symeon Shimin, in 1965. The Story of Passover Text copyright © 1965, 1997 by Norma Simon • Copyright renewed © 1993 by Norma Simon • Illustrations copyright © 1997 by Erika Weihs Printed in the U.S.A. All rights reserved. • Library of Congress Cataloging-in-Publication Data Simon, Norma. The story of Passover / by Norma Simon ; illustrated by Erika Weihs. p. cm. Summary: Describes the origins and traditions of Passover, in particular the special meal called the Seder. ISBN 0-06-027062-4. — ISBN 0-06-027063-2 (lib. bdg.) 1. Passover—Juvenile literature. 2. Seder—Juvenile literature. [1. Passover. 2. Seder.] I. Weihs, Erika, ill. II. Title. BM695.P3S54 1997 95-41201 296.4′37—dc20 CIP AC Typography by David Neuhaus and Elynn Cohen First Edition
1 3 5 4 2
6 8 7
9 10
❖

THE STORY OF
Passover

arly in spring, all around the world, Jewish families celebrate the holiday of Passover. With songs, poems, and prayers, with food and wine, the ancient story of Passover is told.

Passover begins with a special meal called the Seder and lasts for eight days. Each family has its own Seder traditions. The children know that when they are grown and have their own families, they, too, will make Seders and teach their children the Passover story.

The story of the first Passover is written in the Hebrew Bible. It tells of the time over three thousand years ago when the Jews, who were called Hebrews then, left their homes in Canaan for the land of Egypt. There they tended flocks of sheep and lived in peace with the Egyptians.

The Hebrews prayed to one God, even though the Egyptians prayed to many gods. The Pharaoh, who ruled Egypt, let them worship as they pleased.

When that Pharaoh died, a cruel new Pharaoh came to power. He made the Hebrews slaves and forced them to build cities for him. For many years they carried heavy bricks, stones, and mortar and built great temples and pyramids.

The next Pharaoh was even more cruel. Soon the Hebrews lost almost all hope of becoming free people again. They cried out to God for help.

God chose a brave man, Moses, to lead the Hebrews out of slavery. Moses was not afraid of the Pharaoh. "Let my people go," Moses ordered.

Moses performed many miracles to prove that he had come at God's command. But the Pharaoh refused to believe him.

So God sent plagues to Egypt. Hail fell from the skies and no crops could grow. The waters of the River Nile turned to blood, and the fish died. Frogs, lice, locusts, and flies overran the land. But still the stubborn ruler refused to let the Hebrews leave.

The last plague was the worst of all. In every Egyptian house the eldest son died. The Hebrew sons were spared because Moses had told each family to sacrifice a lamb and smear the blood around the door of the house. The blood was a sign to God that a Hebrew lived there, so God's Angel of Death would pass over the house. This is where the word "Passover" comes from.

On that first Passover night even the mighty Pharaoh lost a son. Saddened, he called Moses to him.

"Rise up, children of Israel, and go," he said at last.

Moses quickly called the Jews together. There was no time to prepare food for the journey. They mixed wheat flour with water and carried the dough in wooden boxes on their shoulders with their other belongings.

When they reached the safety of the desert, they rested awhile. They baked the bread in the hot rays of the sun. The flat, unleavened bread, without yeast to make it rise, was called matzoh.

The Pharaoh's sadness over the death of his son soon turned into anger. He ordered his soldiers to ride their chariots into the desert and capture Moses.

The Hebrews had reached the shore of the Red Sea when they saw the soldiers coming. The water was deep, and there was no way to cross.

With God's help Moses performed another miracle. The waters of the Red Sea parted. The Hebrews walked safely through the sea to the opposite shore, but the Egyptians drowned as the water swept over them.

Then Moses led his people through the wilderness back to the land of Canaan.

Ever since that time the story of the Passover and the exodus, the long journey out of Egypt, has been told over and over again. Some people believe it happened exactly as it is written in the Bible. Others believe that the story has changed in the telling, for it was not written down until a thousand years later. They call it a legend.

People have studied the written records left by the Egyptians, hoping to learn more about Moses and the Passover. However, the Egyptians wrote very little about the Hebrews.

We know that a powerful Pharaoh ruled Egypt when a city called Pithom was built by the Hebrew slaves. The records also tell that the exodus was probably between 1300 and 1250 B.C.

Although the exodus was a small event in Egyptian history, it was a time of great rejoicing for the Hebrews. They were free people once again.

Each year they gave thanks to God for the Passover. In Canaan they prayed in a beautiful temple built by King Solomon. Later, after the temple was destroyed in a war, they worshiped wherever they could.

When at last the temple was rebuilt, there was great excitement. Hebrews traveled from all over the country and put up tents on the hillsides. Thousands of them dressed in white holiday robes and waited their turn to bring a lamb into the temple. The lamb was to remember the lambs sacrificed a long time ago in Egypt. There were singing and music and prayers of thanksgiving and feasting on the sacrificial lambs.

The Hebrews always remained true to one God. Parents taught their prayers, their customs, and their language to their children. Even though many Hebrews left Canaan—or Israel, as it was also called—to make new homes in other countries, they never forgot the Passover.

Today Jewish families live in nearly every country in the world. And for them spring always brings preparations for Passover.

During those eight days no other bread but matzoh, the bread once baked in the desert, may be eaten. The day before the Seder the family searches the house. They make sure not even a tiny crumb of bread baked with yeast is left.

Some Jews have special dishes, glasses, silverware, and pots and pans for use during this holiday only. All other kitchenware is put away.

People buy sweet grape wine to drink at the Seder. They also buy packages of matzoth and other Passover foods.

Not so long ago it was harder to get ready for Passover. Grandfathers fermented grapes and made the sweet wine themselves, as their fathers had done before them.

A week before the holiday, enough matzoth were baked for everyone in the town. The houses with the largest ovens were the bakeries, and there were huge piles of flat, unleavened squares.

The afternoon before the Seder, the best tablecloth is put on the table. A bouquet of spring flowers and candles are placed on the table too.

Silverware and a glass for wine are set beside each place. The glasses will be filled and emptied four times during the Seder, so the children are given very small ones.

The largest wineglass on the table is called the Cup of Elijah. It is for the Biblical prophet Elijah, who is an invisible guest at the Seder. The children like to imagine that the prophet visits their Seder and drinks some of his wine. This is part of the legend of Passover.

Near the head of the table is the Matzoh Cloth. It may be made of plain linen or richly embroidered satin. It holds three matzoth. A large dish called the Seder Plate is filled with foods that remind us of the time in Egypt.

Fathers, mothers, grandfathers, grandmothers, aunts, uncles, friends, and children take their places at the Seder table. Tonight everyone at the table may sit as he wishes. Nobody has to sit straight in his chair. Everyone's chair can be soft with cushions, as a reminder that they are free people.

Beside each plate is a copy of the Haggadah, the Passover book. The Haggadah is a book of questions and answers. The children ask the questions, and the story in the Haggadah gives the answers. Like a play in which all the parts are written down, the Haggadah tells the story of the Passover and the order of the Seder.

Haggadahs in America are usually printed in Hebrew on the right side of the page and in English on the left side. Like all Hebrew books, the Haggadah begins at the place we call the back. The pages are then turned from left to right.

The Seder begins with the blessing of the wine. Then the leader of the Seder breaks the middle matzoh in his Matzoh Cloth in two. He or she wraps the larger piece, called the Afikomen, in a napkin and hides it.

Then the youngest child stands and asks the leader of the Seder the important question: "Why is this night different from all other nights of the year?"

The leader of the Seder reads the answers to the question aloud from the Haggadah. With the telling of the bitterness of slavery under the Egyptians, everyone eats a piece of a bitter herb from the Seder Plate.

Everyone also tastes the charoseth from the Seder Plate. The charoseth is made of grated apples, nuts, cinnamon, and wine. It stands for the mortar used to hold together the bricks and stones of which the Pharaoh's cities were built.

The leader of the Seder tells of the terrible plagues the Egyptians suffered. Everyone takes a drop of wine from his or her cup and puts it on a dish—one drop for each of the ten plagues.

Then the leader points to the roasted bone on the Seder Plate. It is a symbol of the lamb sacrificed for the first Passover.

When the leader repeats the story of Moses and bread baked in the desert, everyone eats a piece of matzoh.

On the Seder Plate, too, are a roasted egg and some parsley. The egg stands for the Seder feast that will follow, and the parsley for the new hope spring brings to the hearts of all people.

Next, the Seder feast is served. The delicious food is eaten slowly, for no one may order a free person to hurry.

During the Seder some of the children find the hidden Afikomen and keep it. Then, when the leader of the Seder looks for it, they giggle and the grown-ups pretend to be upset. The Afikomen is needed to finish the Seder.

The children promise to return it if they are given gifts. After agreeing happily, the leader shares the Afikomen with everyone at the table to remember the lambs sacrificed at the temple in Jerusalem for Passover. The roasted lambs were shared in the Seder feast.

The Seder ends with singing. The songs ring through the house as they once rang out in King Solomon's temple. The children love the songs and often know them by heart.

During the other days of Passover, the Song of Solomon is read from the Bible. Stories of last year's Seder are told, and the children may ask their grandparents to tell about Passover when they were children. There is a mixture of memories in every family's Passover.

For Passover meals there are light, fluffy dumplings made of matzoh-meal flour and eggs. Sometimes soft, yellow sponge cakes are baked. Some families eat thin matzoh-meal pancakes with sugar and jelly on top. For lunch there are often crisp matzoh sandwiches.

Today in Israel, the homeland of the Jewish people, the first harvest of the year has been gathered by Passover.

Jerusalem, the capital city, is filled with Israeli travelers. Other Jews travel long distances to be with their families and friends for the holiday.

Israeli citizens have come to Israel from many places. Often they escaped from war and persecution to the safety of Israel. The stories of their flights are told at Israeli Seders.

Before the Civil War in the United States, the story of Moses leading his people out of Egypt gave hope and comfort to the African-American slaves. They sang a song of freedom called "Go Down, Moses." It uses the words Moses spoke to the Pharaoh, "Let my people go."

Slavery has been a part of the human story since before history began. Passover celebrates the Hebrews' escape from slavery and the right of all people to be free. Each time Jewish children hear the story of Moses and the exodus, they learn how important freedom is, not only for Jews but for all people.

Things to Make for Passover

Please ask an adult to help you make these delicious foods for Passover.

Matzoh Balls

(makes about 25 matzoh balls)

Ingredients:

3 eggs

1 tablespoon vegetable oil

½ teaspoon salt

dash of pepper

1 tablespoon dried or fresh parsley

½ cup matzoh meal

1½ quarts slightly salted water or chicken soup

Separate the eggs, whites in one bowl and yolks in another. First, beat egg whites until stiff. Next, beat yolks until pale yellow and bubbly. Blend oil, salt, pepper, and parsley into beaten egg yolks. Using a spatula, fold the egg-yolk mixture into the stiff egg whites. Then, one spoonful at a time, gradually fold the matzoh meal into the egg mixture. After the matzoh meal is completely folded into the egg mixture, cover and refrigerate for 1 hour or more.

Fill a large pot with the slightly salted water or chicken soup and bring to a rolling boil. Next, take batter out of the refrigerator. Wet your hands and shape small balls out of the batter, a little smaller than golf balls. Drop the balls into the boiling water (or soup). Cover the pot and let the matzoh balls simmer slowly for 30 to 40 minutes. Test one ball to be sure it is soft all the way through. Serve 2–3 matzoh balls in a bowl of hot chicken soup for the Seder. Enjoy!

Charoseth

Charoseth is the Passover symbol of the mortar and bricks the Hebrews were forced to use when they were slaves in Egypt. The Hebrews helped to build pyramids and cities for the Egyptians. The sweetness of the charoseth reminds us of the sweet promise of a better world for all people.

Ingredients:

2–3 large, firm apples (such as Granny Smith), peeled and cored

½ cup walnuts

¼ cup sweet red wine or grape juice

½ teaspoon cinnamon (or more, to taste)

1 teaspoon honey (or more, to taste)

Put the apples and walnuts in a food processor or blender and process until the pieces are coarsely chopped. (You can also use a hand-held grater and nut grinder.) Add wine, cinnamon, and honey, and blend all the ingredients together until they form a rough paste. Taste it. Add more cinnamon and/or honey if desired.

Serve in a small dish on the traditional Seder Plate. Use during the Seder.

Leftover charoseth is delicious on matzoh or crackers. You can also mix it with yogurt to make a tasty Passover treat!

This recipe serves 8–10 people for the Seder with leftovers.

Passover place cards

Welcome each person to the Seder table with a decorated place card. You will need:

> a list of guest and family names
> pieces of paper approximately 4 inches by 4 inches
> crayons or colored pencils or felt-tip pens

Fold one piece of paper in half for each name—each place card should stand up. Decorate the cards with Passover designs: spring leaves, flowers, matzoth, grapes or grapevines, Egyptian designs, stick figures of Hebrews leaving Egypt, lambs, or the Star of David. Place the cards on the Seder table. Your guests will love to have their own hand-decorated cards on this very special night.

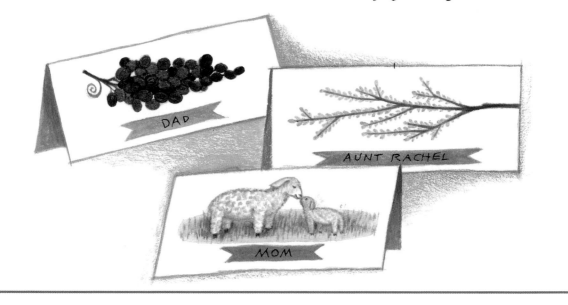